FIFE
INDEPENDENTS

DAVID DEVOY

AMBERLEY

First published 2017

Amberley Publishing
The Hill, Stroud
Gloucestershire, GL5 4EP

www.amberley-books.com

ISBN 978 1 4456 6596 2 (print)
ISBN 978 1 4456 6597 9 (ebook)

British Library Cataloguing in Publication Data.
A catalogue record for this book is available from
the British Library.

Typesetting by Amberley Publishing.
Printed in the UK.

Setting the Scene

In the early years of the twentieth century almost every bus and coach operator was "Independent", unless owned by the local council or operated with a large shareholding owned by the railways. As the years went by more and more companies succumbed to take-over offers from these larger and well-funded operators. In Fife the largest operator was Walter Alexander who continued after The Scottish Motor Traction Company acquired the shares. SMT was in turn funded by two mainline railway companies. Alexanders had been purchasing shares in some of the locally owned bus companies and merged two of these in 1929 as Simpson's & Forrester's, and this ran until being fully absorbed in 1938. As part of this deal Frank Simpson was employed by Alexander's and ran the garage premises at Dunfermline Market Street until his death in June 1961, after which the buses were transferred to St Leonards Garage in Dunfermline. Other services were added in the 1930s with the acquisition of Scottish General (Northern) Omnibus Co., the bus services operated by the Dunfermline & District Tramways Co., and the General Motor Carrying Company of Kirkcaldy. The last major competitor was eliminated in Fife when Alexander's buses replaced the tram network formerly operated by Kirkcaldy Corporation in 1931.

In 1948 the mainline railway companies were nationalised; this meant the state now owned a large part of the SMT Group. Full control was obtained the following year when the remaining shares were added. Things continued almost unchanged until 1961, when it was decided to split the Alexander Co. into three more manageable units. For Fife this meant that 516 buses were transferred to a new company formed as W. Alexander & Sons (Fife) Ltd. A new livery of Ayres Red replaced the blue formerly carried in the Kingdom of Fife in 1962. The Forth Road Bridge was opened in 1964, allowing access to what had been a difficult part of Scotland to reach, and linked Fife to Edinburgh and beyond. The Kingdom contained no major stage carriage operators, but a few little companies were mopped up in the 1960s. Fleming of Anstruther was bought out in 1965; T. D. Niven of St Andrews in 1967; and R. Drydale of Cupar followed at the end of 1967. The Alexander Co. later traded as Fife Scottish, and is currently owned by the Stagecoach Group, trading as Stagecoach Fife, and Rennie's.

Private hire and contracts were fair game for the independents remaining, and new operators sprang up over the years. The coal mining industry alone once employed 25,000 men. When the Forth and Tay rail bridges opened, linking Fife with Dundee to the north and Edinburgh to the south, the county boomed. Ports were constructed in Methil, Burntisland and Rosyth. Rosyth Dockyard is a large naval dockyard on the Firth of Forth at Rosyth, which formerly undertook refitting of Royal Navy surface vessels and submarines. Kirkcaldy was the world leader for production of linoleum and, latterly, high tech companies moved to the new town of Glenrothes, taking advantage of an available workforce due to the decline of the coal mining industry.

In the 1970s the major operator Alexander (Fife) began to lose valuable private-hire work due to a lack of suitable vehicles. Its policy of specifying dual-purpose vehicles made its coaches look inferior to the independents, and a lack of staff willing to work at weekends did not help either. The privately owned firms steadily built up fine fleets of coaches, and were more willing to provide double-deckers for schools and contract work. Their use of part-time staff also helped win business at busy times. There was dissatisfaction with the services being run by Alexander Fife and several independents tried to obtain a share of service work. Raymond Abercrombie applied for a service in Glenrothes in 1971, and Rennie's also tried for a local service in Dunfermline the same year. Neither was successful.

A major event in the early 1980s occurred, during a time when most of the British bus network was in public ownership, which in Scotland meant the state-owned Scottish Bus Group. It was regulated, with operators not subject to competition. The Thatcher government commissioned a white paper into the bus industry. This resulted in the implementation of the Transport Act 1985 on 26 October 1986 and the deregulation of bus services in England, Scotland and Wales. The Act abolished road service licensing and allowed for the introduction of competition on local bus services for the first time since the 1930s. To operate a service, all an accredited operator was required to do was provide fifty-six days' notice to the Traffic Commissioner of their intention to commence, cease or alter operation on a route. Almost immediately existing operators faced competition on their most profitable routes, both from new and existing operators. This would often result in the incumbent operator retaliating by starting up operations on the new operator's home turf. Tactics included cutting fares and operating extra services.

The major independents in the Kingdom included Rennie's Lion Coaches, which were established in 1947 as a family-owned company based in Dunfermline. 1963 saw the takeover of Comfort Coaches of Dunfermline, which added a further half-dozen vehicles. The new business traded as Rennie's Lion and Comfort Coaches, but thankfully this was simplified in 1974 to Rennie's of Dunfermline Ltd. An express service commenced linking Dunfermline and Rosyth to Plymouth, which was intended mainly for Naval personnel. A new depot was built at Cairneyhill in 1971. Interesting service applications in 1974 were for a Glasgow–Frankfurt and Glasgow–Amsterdam route, but these were later withdrawn. 1975 saw the takeover of King's of Dunblane, adding around six coaches to the fleet. Charlie King later took back full control. During 1987 a huge fleet of Atlanteans, Metropolitans, Nationals and Dominators was steadily building up, reaching a fleet total of around eighty buses by the end of the year. A network of local services that competed with Fife Scottish was launched from January 1988 onwards. Fife responded by introducing minibuses on some routes. Operations were moved to more spacious premises at Wellwood, north of Dunfermline in October 1988. Disaster struck from 16th April 1990, after the commercial network was expanded. Drivers struggled to meet running times with the elderly vehicles being used on many routes, and absenteeism reached epidemic proportions. The company withdrew most of the network overnight on 25 April and around fifty employees lost their jobs. The fleet was reduced from around eighty to just fifty-five, and the emphasis was on private hire and contracts once more. By 25 September all service work had ceased. Following the retirement of Jack Rennie in 2008, the business was sold to Stagecoach East

Scotland; Rennie's continues to operate as a separate business, although no longer classed as an independent.

Another business founded around the same time was Wilmax Motorways of Methil, owned by the Williamson Family (not to be confused with Williamson's of Gauldry). From 1966 it decided to trade as Kingdom Coaches of Methil instead.

Jack's of Oakley has come and gone a few times, often running minibuses. Major expansion occurred when contracts were obtained for the building of ExxonMobil Chemical's Fife Ethylene Plant at Mossmorran, 25 miles north of Edinburgh. The end of this circa 1985/6 led to the business contracting and eventually ceasing all together.

James Moffat of Cardenden established his company in 1950 and, by the time of his death in 1975 at age sixty-five, he had built up a fleet of fifty vehicles. This included coaches, lorries and bulk liquid carriers. Moffat & Williamson Ltd was formed by the amalgamation of James Moffat & Sons of Cardenden and Williamson's of Gauldry, who began operations in 1945. The two companies joined forces in 1978 to operate from depots in Gauldry and Cardenden in Fife. Williamson's had operated services from Gauldry to Newport, and from Dundee to Tealing, up until 1966. Applications were made to join these routes together by using the new Forth Road Bridge but were unsuccessful, as was a proposed service linking Dundee to Tayport and Wormit. A second depot was opened at Leslie in 1973, but a fire in January 1980 led to its closure. In 1980 a brand-new depot was built at Glenrothes to replace both Leslie and Cardenden, and the Moffat family ceased to have any input with the company after 1981. In late 1987 the fleet was increased to allow for a network of services to be introduced. Ironically much of the painting was contracted to SBG Engineering and done at the former workshops of Fife Scottish. Services were steadily built up from 1988, many competing with Fife Scottish. When control of Fife was obtained by Stagecoach Holdings in July 1991, a more aggressive stance was taken by the new owners and heavy competition ensued, with tendered journeys operated by M&W being registered against. The smaller firm complained to the Office of Fair Trading that Stagecoach were competing in an anti-competitive manner. Sadly in July 1994 the company withdrew almost all its commercial services throughout Fife, including the St Andrews–Dundee service. The OFT told Fife Scottish to clean up its act, and it did. Unfortunately it was too late for M&W, who were losing an estimated £50,000 a year, and had to cut their fleet from ninety-four to around fifty-four buses as a result. A small-scale network of services remains to this day. Gauldry depot and workshops were closed in December 2005 after new facilities were added to the yard at St Fort. The Williamson family relinquished control in June 2012, when the business was sold to its managing director George Devine, who along with his wife Ann became the new directors.

Bay Travel was started in 2008 by Vincent Derighetti and Iain Robertson, when they decided to match up Vincent's extensive business experience with Iain's equally extensive knowledge of the coach industry. Since then, the company has expanded rapidly, and the two partners are now operating an expanding quality fleet of vehicles, all round Scotland and further afield. As well as being a quality private-hire and tour operator, Bay Travel also operate a number of local services and school contracts.

A1 Minibus & Coach Services Ltd was established in 1979 by the late Ian Goodsir. Ian started out in Methilhill with one eight-seater minibus doing a local service contract for Fife Council. One of his hobbies was Greyhound racing; both he and his wife Isobel attended Thornton Greyhound racing track on a weekly basis. One evening Ian was lucky to get a decent win at the greyhounds and decided to buy himself a minibus with his winnings, which is where his journey began. The business began to grow reasonably quickly, as Ian decided to introduce coaches to his fleet and managed to secure contracts to keep the wheels turning. His sons later joined the business – David as transport manager, Kenny as a mechanic and youngest son Ian as a driver. As the years have gone by, the business has gone from strength to strength and they now have a fleet of around sixty-two vehicles with fifty-two employees.

Allison's of Dunfermline were a coach operator from the 1970s, who later branched into service work, although some were only evening and Sunday journeys. Former Fife Scottish Burntisland local service 7 and the Glenrothes–Leven service 47 were taken over from April 1990. Tendered services linking Abbeyfield to Dunfermline General Hospital were added from March 1992, and some service 14B journeys between Dunfermline and Cairneyhill followed in 1994. In 1997 the firm won a major contract for school transport and fifteen double-deckers were purchased. 1998 saw more gains, with the following services all added: service 81 Dunfermline–Dalgety Bay, service 17A Cowdenbeath–Kelty, service 28 Dunfermline–Kincardine–Falkirk, Service 58B Glenrothes–Queen Margaret Hospital in Dunfermline, service 76 Wellwood–Crombie, and service 82 Inverkeithing–Dunfermline. The company was on the verge of purchasing new service buses when Stagecoach put in an attractive offer to sell out, and the firm was taken over in April 2000.

Established coach operator Armstong's of Inverkeithing had a go in March 1987 with a couple of routes around Dunfermline; they used Leyland Nationals, but de-registered them in June the same year. Glenrothes mini-coaches operated a short-lived route in Glenrothes between Woodside and Balgeddie.

Black's of Lochgelly were involved in private hire and contract work until August 1991, when some tendered services were taken over from Fife Scottish. Service 17A from Kelty to Cowdenbeath, and some early morning journeys on service 19 Ballingry to Dunfermline were operated for a while. Evening and Sunday journeys linking Stirling and St Andrews followed in January 1992.

Anderson's of Lower Largo were also involved in tendered services, operating the 61A service linking St Andrews and Earlsferry. New Gilston–Anstruther and New Gilston–Auchtermuchty routes were later added.

George Gallagher trading as Orion Omnibus Transport Ltd, based in Mitchelston Industrial Estate in Kirkcaldy, started clockwise and anticlockwise circular services linking Kirkcaldy, Burntisland, Dalgety Bay, Dunfermline, Cowdenbeath, Lochgelly and Cardenden in February 1993, numbered B1 and B1A. Stagecoach responded fiercely with similar routes and, by June 1993, his business had ceased.

Gordon's of Leslie started as a coach hirer in 1981, and has continued to build up the business. Tendered services were introduced in August 1997 between Dunfermline and Stratheden Hospital and from High Valleyfield to Cairneyhill. 1998 saw service 65B linking Ladybank and Newburgh taken over.

Donald of Cupar tried a Cupar–Dundee service number 66 from January to April 2004, partly serving roads not served by Stagecoach. Donaldson of St Andrews traded as North Fife Travel before adopting the St Andrews Executive Travel identity, although the legal name of the company wasn't changed until March 2011.

Malcolm of Cowdenbeath later traded Taphaul Coaches and then launched Premier Travel. A loose alliance was formed with Davies of Plean and Myles of Plean, in which they would all use the same name and could lend each other vehicles, but it didn't last long. Premier Travel then rather bizarrely traded as West Coast Coaches, even though based in the east of Scotland.

In 1988 Rennie's purchased a batch of fifty-five Leyland Atlanteans from Strathclyde Buses. Around eighteen were kept and the rest were resold but, interestingly, it was the older buses that remained, probably due to the fact that the bodywork was of a better build quality. NGB 117M was originally Greater Glasgow PTE LA749, and dates from October 1973.

YN09 HRK was a Volvo B12BT/Plaxton Elite C57FT, purchased new by Logan of Dunloy in May 2009. It joined Moffat & Williamson in December 2012, and was re-registered to FSU 374. It was snapped in Glasgow while working on a private hire.

YN53 GGO was a Scania Omnicity CN94UB B42F, new as Menzies Aviation, Heathrow Airport number T55 in October 2003. It is shown in Dunfermline with Bay Travel of Cowdenbeath while working on the 89 service to Crossford. The single-deck OmniCity was first introduced in 2002 in right-hand drive for the UK market. Unlike the Scania L94UB and OmniLink, the OmniCity features a full low floor without the need for steps or ramps to reach the rear seats, similar to the Volvo B7L.

M699 HBC was a Dennis Javelin 12SDA/Plaxton Premiere 350 C49Ft, new to Smart & Howieson of Newburgh in August 1994. The firm traded under the name of Abbey Coaches and ran a fleet of around half a dozen coaches at any given time on a mixture of contracts and private hires. It would later run for P. W. Jones of Hereford and Pilkington's of Accrington.

F357 TSX was a Mercedes Benz 811D/Alexander C33F, purchased new by Carr's of Whitburn in July 1989. It joined Anderson of Lower Largo the following year. It was working on service 61A, which linked St Andrews to Earlsferry, and was loading in South Street. It would later pass to Evan's of Heswall and McNairn's of Coatbridge for further service.

A115 XNH was a Volvo B10M-61/Jonckheere Jubilee CH49/9Dt, delivered new to Scotts Greys of Darlington in April 1984. It is shown with M. Bruce trading as St Andrews Coaches on a private hire to Glasgow, and had been re-registered as FIL 4910 in October 1988. Jonckheere celebrated its first century in business in 1981 with a touring coach given the appropriate name of Jubilee; these were built at Roeselare in Belgium.

In 1976 Rennie's caused quite a stir when they purchased TLS 733P. It was a one-off intermediate-length Leyland National, which was built from half a 10.3-metre and half an 11.3-metre model. It was fitted with coach seats and used on a run from Kinross to Methil. It later became number 13 in the Fishwick of Leyland fleet.

BV55 XYR was a MAN 18.350/Beaulas C49Ft originally registered as 06-KK-1451 in Ireland. It came to A1 Coaches of Methil from Holmeswood Coaches and carried the registration number RSU 498 for a while. It has also been operated by Festival Travel. A1 Coaches were only formed in 1979 and have steadily built up their business since then.

ASC 680B was a Leyland Titan PD3/6/Alexander H41/29F, purchased new by Edinburgh Corporation as their fleetnumber 680 in September 1964. It passed to Williamson's of Gauldry in 1977 with another five similar vehicles, and was initially used in Lothian livery. The bus is seen at Gauldry depot, freshly repainted into the brown version of the livery favoured by Moffat's, but carries M & W fleetnames.

OSR 894R was a Ford R1114/Plaxton Supreme C53F, purchased new by Williamson of Methil, trading as Kingdom Coaches, in March 1977. The mustard livery was adopted in the 1960s and normally around four coaches were operated at any time. The use of lightweight vehicles meant that they were cheaper to purchase and could be traded in after a few years, keeping a modern look to the fleet.

FGE 428X was a Dennis Dominator DD137B/Alexander RL Type H45/34F, new as Central Scottish number D28 in June 1982. It was transferred to Kelvin Scottish as their number 1722, and later became a member of the Kelvin Central Buses fleet. It passed to Moffat & Williamson in 1997, and was captured near St Andrews.

JDS 645N was a Ford R1114/Duple Dominant C53F, purchased new by Williamson's of Gauldry in April 1975. It carries the traditional Williamson's blue livery. After the merger with Moffat's, the new company unusually kept both Moffat's brown and Williamson's blue, with a proportion of vehicles receiving each livery. Eventually an improved version of Moffat's brown was applied, with orange on a cream base.

WTN 641H was a Leyland Atlantean PDR2/1/Alexander J Type H48/30D, new as Tyne & Wear PTE number 641 in January 1970. It passed to Rennie's and was used extensively before sale to Jock Sturrock of Kirkcaldy, who utilised it on bingo contracts. The Atlantean was manufactured by Leyland Motors between 1958 and 1986.

JPA 104K was an AEC Reliance 6U2R/Park Royal DP45F, new in December 1971, and was previously London Country RP4. It was one of ninety new to London Country for Green Line express work. It is shown in Dunfermline bus station. On disposal it would pass to Jack Waddell of Lochwinnoch, and later Marbill Travel of Beith. Park Royal Vehicles was one of Britain's leading coachbuilders and bus manufacturers, based at Park Royal, West London. Sadly it was closed down in July 1980.

OSG 545M was a Leyland Leopard PSU3/3R/Alexander Y Type C49F, new as Eastern Scottish number ZH545 in January 1974, and passed to Alexander (Midland) the following year as their MPE225. It is seen with Hall's of Kennoway, working their Saturday service linking Anstruther Holiday Park and Glasgow.

PSP 166J was a Bedford VAS5/Plaxton C29F, purchased new by Toolan of Kinglassie in March 1971. It would later pass to J. K. Moffat of Leven before joining Short, trading as Glenrothes Mini-Coaches. It was snapped on a visit to Balloch. Short ran a circular service in Glenrothes in 1986.

565 CRW was a Daimler Fleetline CRG66LX/Alexander H78F, new in September 1963 as a Daimler demonstrator. It was purchased by Graham's Bus Service of Paisley in August 1967 as number 75 and later D2. It passed to Paul Sykes of Barnsley (dealer) in May 1979 and then went to Moffat & Williamson in July 1979. It was photographed on a football hire to Ibrox Park in Glasgow in 1980 and it would remain in service until August 1983.

In 1979 Van Hool McArdle closed their factory at Spa Road in Dublin. A number of incomplete bodies and parts remained in stock, so Silverdale Coaches of Dublin had enough parts to assemble six of these '300 series' bodies. This Bedford YMT/Silverdale C53F was imported unused from Eire for Grufferty of Horden and registered as NDC 284W in May 1981. It then ran for Alexandra Coaches of Sunderland as C49Ft. It then passed to Blair & Palmer of Carlisle before joining Rennie's of Dunfermline in March 1985, where it is seen here. It was caught in Cairneyhill on a cold winter's day.

A657 EMY was a Leyland Royal Tiger RT B54-65/Roe Doyen C47Ft, new to
National Travel (London) in June 1984. On disposal, it joined the fleet of Hughes
Bros of Llandudno, trading as Alpine, later passing to Hall's of Kennoway in 1993,
where it became GBZ 4991. It was re-registered to A939 XGG and passed to Spencer
of Leven in 1994, but was burnt out in a depot fire in October 2000.

YBK 341V was a Leyland Atlantean AN68A/1R/Alexander AL Type H45/28D, new
as Portsmouth Corporation number 341 in November 1979. It briefly passed to
Stagecoach with the business, but Stagecoach was forced to re-sell the company by the
Office of Fair Trading. The new owners were Transit Holdings. Moffat & Williamson
purchased ten of these buses from Thames Transit in 1991.

HSD 706N was a Volvo B58-61/Alexander M Type C42Ft, purchased new by Western SMT as their V2535 in May 1975. On disposal it passed to Hall's of Kennoway, where this replacement front panel was fitted from a Plaxton Supreme. It was re-registered as OSL44N upon its disposal. The low second-hand prices obtained for these buses led to SBG rebuilding many later Duple coaches before disposal, as the small windows lessened their appeal to prospective buyers.

HTX 729N was a Leyland National 11351/1R B49F, purchased new by Merthyr Tydfil as their fleetnumber 198. It was acquired by Rennie's in 1987 for use on the expanding network of services being built up in Fife, but was sold the following year to People's Provincial and allocated fleetnumber 397.

USR 394S was a Bedford CFL/Reeve Burgess C17F, purchased new by Williamson's of Gauldry in May 1978. Harry Reeve set up in Pilsley as a blacksmith and coachbuilder. In 1925 the company was formed into a partnership with George Kenning and became Reeve & Kenning Ltd. In 1958 the Kenning family interest was bought by the Reeve family. In 1974 the firm passed to T. H. Burgess Holdings of Worcester and the name was changed to Reeve Burgess Ltd. In 1980 the company became part of the Plaxton Group based in Scarborough.

A77 RGE was a Ford T152/Plaxton Paramount C35F, purchased new by Reekie of Kinglassie in November 1983. The chassis was a standard factory-length Ford R1115 (i.e., 11 metres long with a 150-bhp engine) that had been shortened by Tricentrol Trucks to provide a shorter-length coach. In an attempt to lower the floor height of the vehicle, the turbocharged diesel engine was tilted over to one side circa 1978. Synchromesh transmission was fitted as standard but some later examples were equipped with Allison automatic gearboxes.

LK03 NKC was a Transbus Trident H39/20D, purchased new by Centrewest as their fleetnumber TN1277 in April 2003. It passed to Bay Travel, and was snapped in its home town of Cowdenbeath while working on the 17C service that links Crossgates to Cowdenbeath and Kelty. The advert for D&G Autocare is very effective; the firm now has fourteen garages, including six in Fife.

JSF 774T was a Bedford YMT/Plaxton Supreme C46F, new to Silver Fox Coaches of Edinburgh in December 1978. It passed to Anstruther Coaches before joining Moffat & Williamson; it was a strange acquisition, as M&W were really heavyweight operators at the time. Possibly it was obtained with some work. It was not destined to remain long, however, and quickly passed to Peter Irvine of Law and was re-registered as TFG154.

BSN 465V was a Bedford YMT/Unicar C53F, purchased new by J. K. Moffat of Leven in September 1979; it is seen in Glasgow's Bellahouston Park on a hire. Spanish-built Unicar coachwork bodies were available on Bedford YMT coach chassis from January 1979. Union Carrocera appointed Moseley Group (PSV) Ltd as its sole UK concessionaire for the model, which made its British debut at the Brighton Coach Rally this year in 1978.

612 UKM was a Leyland Atlantean PDR1/1/Weymann H44/33F, purchased new by Maidstone & District (DH612) in March 1963. It was sold to Bristol Omnibus and used as an open topper at Weston-super-Mare, later passing to Badgerline. It is shown here with Hall of Kennoway under the Forth Rail Bridge. On disposal, it joined London Bus Exports and was exported abroad.

NKU 150X was a Dennis Dominator DDA133/Alexander RH Type H46/32F, new as South Yorkshire PTE number 2150 in December 1981. It is seen in Mainline livery after purchase by Allison's of Dunfermline, leaving the Stagecoach depot in Cowdenbeath. This depot was vacated by Stagecoach Fife, but is expected to be the new base for the Rennie's fleet.

KUM 540L was a Leyland Leopard PSU3B/4R/Plaxton Elite C53F, new to Wallace Arnold subsidiary Woburn Garage, WC1, in April 1973. On disposal it became Wombwell Coaches number 102, before reaching Jack's of Cowdenbeath. It would later pass to Rennie's for further service. Jack's originally traded as Jack's of Oakley, and stopped and resumed operations a couple of times over the years.

PSF 224P was a Bedford YMT/Duple Dominant C53F, purchased new by Lothian Regional Transport in July 1976 for use on city tours and hires. It is seen with Armstrong's of Inverkeithing on a hire to the Glasgow Garden Festival.

YHA 298J was a Ford R192/Plaxton Derwent B45F, purchased new by Midland Red in November 1970 as their number 6298. It passed to Moffat & Williamson in August 1978 before joining A&C McLennan of Spittlefield in June 1980. It lasted until April 1985, when it was withdrawn. It actually passed to Stagecoach with the business in April 1986, although it was a non-runner.

OCD 775 was a Leyland Titan PD2/12/Park Royal H31/26RD, purchased new by Southdown as their fleetnumber 775 in May 1955. It leads a line of Titan's outside Rennie's Cairneyhill depot. This chassis featured the Leyland O.600 engine, which was named after its displacement in cubic inches; the 'O' standing for oil. The 600 cubic inch swept volume equated to 9.8 litres.

OWK 662W was a Ford 'A' Series / Moseley Faro II C21F shown with Hendry's of Glenrothes. The town was planned in the late 1940s as one of Scotland's first post-Second World War new towns. It developed as an important industrial centre in Scotland's Silicon Glen between 1961 and 2000 with several major electronics and hi-tech companies setting up facilities in the town.

E155 XHS was a Volvo B10M-61/Duple 320 C55F, purchased new by Hutchison's of Overtown in January 1988. It was re-registered as KSK 934 in 1995, and became E497 CHS on disposal. It joined the fleet of J&S Anderson of Lower Largo in January 1996, and is seen in Methil. By 2003, it had moved on to A. C. Williams of Ancaster.

WTN 646H was a Leyland Atlantean PDR2/1/Alexander J Type H48/30D, purchased new by Tyne & Wear PTE as their number 646 in January 1970. It passed to Rennie's of Dunfermline and was freshly placed into service when snapped at Cairneyhill. Production of the J type, double-deck body (for Leyland Atlantean/Daimler Fleetline) continued until 1972.

APH 516T was a Volvo B58-61/Duple Dominant II C53F, purchased new by Hodge of Sandhurst in March 1979. It passed to Howieson & Smart, trading as Abbey Garage of Newburgh. It later joined Grayline of Bicester and was re-registered as KIB 7026. The Duple Dominant was built by Duple between 1972 and 1982 with an all-steel structure. The Dominant II was introduced in 1976 and had a deeper windscreen, rectangular headlights and a flat rear window.

UFG 58S was a Leyland National 11351A/2R B44D, new as Southdown number 58 in September 1977. It passed to Brighton and Hove, then Gem Fairtax, then London and Country, before reaching Allison's of Dunfermline. The red-and-yellow livery was adopted after some buses were bought from Clydeside 2000.

Y38 TSJ was a Bova Futura FHD12-370 C49Ft, purchased new by Beaton's of Blantyre in March 2001. It passed to Hamish Gordon of Leslie in May 2005, and received the very apt registration R8OVA. It was captured on a hire to the Braehead Xscape Adventure Centre in Renfrew. Gordon's usually operate around eleven vehicles at any given time.

VNB 169L was a Leyland Atlantean AN68/1R/Park Royal H43/32F, new as SELNEC 7069 in February 1973. On disposal, it passed to Skill's of Nottingham before purchase by Moffat & Williamson in 1988. It was working a local service in Glenrothes. It would see further service with Hall's of Kennoway.

A730 HFP was a Volvo B10M-61/Duple Caribbean C51F, purchased new by Park's of Hamilton in March 1984. On disposal in 1986 it joined Redden, trading as French of Coldingham, before reaching Robert Toolan of Kinglassie in 1998. It was passing through Cowdenbeath when snapped.

STD 179L was a Leyland Atlantean AN68/1R/East Lancs H43/31F, purchased new by Fishwick of Leyland as their number 17 in October 1972. It passed to Rennie's of Dunfermline and was on a Dunfermline school contract. It later joined Edwards of Llantwit Fardre for further service.

LK03 NKX was a Transbus Trident H39/20D, new as Centrewest TN1288 in May 2003. It joined Metroline with Firstbus London operations, but now works in Fife for Moffat & Williamson. So far the four buses in this batch have retained their London red livery.

Former Lothian Dennis Trident/Plaxton President SN51 AXU has been repainted in this blue-based livery, which has not been adopted for the rest of the fleet and remains a one-off. It was captured in Cowdenbeath High Street working on the busy 17 service.

900 EVT was a Daimler CVD6-30/Northern Counties H39/30F, new as Potteries Motor Traction number H8900 in November 1958. Its engine was converted to a Leyland 0600 unit by PMT. On disposal it passed to Allander Travel of Milngavie, before joining Rennie's fleet in 1973. It was resold the following year to Silverline Coaches of Thornliebank, Glasgow.

Y149 HWE was a Neoplan N316SHD C53F, delivered new to Stainton Holidays of Kendal in July 2001. It was re-registered as A4FWS for a time before returning to its original plate. It joined MacMillan of Charlestown, trading as Living High Travel, in December 2005, and received the cherished plate K10 LHT. It was heading along Princes Street in Edinburgh.

UUM 624M was a Bedford YRT/Plaxton Elite C53F, purchased new by Wildman of Horsforth in June 1974. It passed to Carney's of Sunderland, before reaching Jack's of Cowdenbeath, and was snapped on a visit to Glasgow.

WAL 121 was a Leyland Titan PD3/4/Weymann L35/32RD, delivered new to East Midland as their number D121 in July 1957. It is shown working for Rennie's on a school contract in Dunfermline, but would pass to Park's of Hamilton for further service.

EJR 115W was a Leyland Atlantean AN68C/2R/Alexander AL Type DPH45/33F, new as Tyne & Wear PTE number 115 in December 1980. It was re-seated to H49/37F and joined Moffat & Williamson in 1999. The location was Glenrothes, and it would later see further service with McLean's of Airdrie.

VSP 967L was a Leyland Leopard PSU5/4R/Van Hool Vistadome C44Ft, purchased new by Rennie's of Dunfermline in May 1973. It was the flagship of the fleet and intended for use on the Plymouth– Rosyth express service, featuring a ten-speed pneumocyclic gearbox, reclining seats and a galley. After disposal it was, surprisingly, repurchased for a second time from O'Neil's of Greenock and re-registered as 439 BUS.

YHA 262J was a Daimler Fleetline CRG6 LXB/Alexander J Type H75D, delivered new to Midland Red as their 6262 in January 1971. It passed with BMMO's Birmingham area operations to West Midlands PTE, where it was rebuilt to be single door before its disposal to Moffat & Williamson. It was photographed at the old depot in Gauldry. BMMO specified flat glass for the windscreens. It would later pass to Baker's of Weston-super-Mare.

B353 YGG was a DAF MB200/Van Hool Alizee C49Ft, purchased new by Euroline of Birkenhead in September 1984, later becoming 4730EL. It was bought by Reekie of Kinglassie in 1988 as B321 EGE. The Alizee body was launched in 1978 and remained in production until the late 1990s.

MW08 BUS was a MAN 14.240/MCV Evolution B43F, delivered new to Moffat & Williamson in March 2008 and shown at work in Glenrothes. On disposal it passed to WJC Buses of Chapelhall and was re-registered as WJ08 BUS. It was later exported to New Zealand for further service.

T734 ASR was a Bova Futura FHD12-340 C49Ft, purchased new by Alex Henderson of Glenrothes, trading as Scotia Travel, in March 1999. It is shown on a hire to Glasgow. It had been re-registered as WFE36 by the time of this photograph, however.

KWY 236P was a rare beast. It was a Mercedes-Benz LP0608/Plaxton Supreme C29F, new to Mercedes-Benz, Brentford, for use as a demonstrator. It is seen later in its life with Bruce of Pitscottie, a Fife-based operator from the St Andrews area, at Glasgow's Bellahouston Park during a World Pipe Band Championships Contest. It would later pass to Meffan's of Kirriemuir and MacEwan's of Dumfries.

Seen between duties at Dunfermline bus station, OTN 459R was a Scania BR111DH MCW Metropolitan H75F. They were very fast, but also very thirsty vehicles. Most had quite short lives as they tended to rust quite badly, but MCW learned many lessons from this that were incorporated in the later Metrobus models. It had begun life as Tyne & Wear PTE number 459 in July 1977.

SK52 OJH was a Dennis Dart SLF/Plaxton Pointer B42F, new as Lothian Buses number 64 in December 2002. It is shown with leading Fife independent Bay Travel, who are steadily improving their fleet, and is loading at Dunfermline bus station.

J600 JFJ was VDL SB120/Plaxton Centro B39F, purchased new by Johnson of Brae in March 2006. On disposal it was re-registered as YO06 TXF, and is seen with subsequent owners Moffat & Williamson at Glenrothes, leaving for Markinch.

D50 OWJ was an MCW Metroliner HR131/9 C50Ft, delivered new to East Midland as their number 50 in October 1996. It was acquired by Selwyn's of Runcorn before purchase by Hall's of Kennoway in March 1993, and was re-registered as GBZ4991. On disposal it joined Robert's of Bridgend, then Bygone Tours in Kent.

A number of former Devon General Bristol VR/ECWs were acquired by Moffat & Williamson in 1987. Included in these were a trio of buses that were new to Oxford South Midland. Former Devon General 964 (GUD 751N) started life as City of Oxford 439. Sister bus OUP 679P was new as United Automobile 679 in May 1976.

A522 LCX was a Ford R1114/Duple Dominant IV C53F, purchased new by Jack's of Dunfermline in September 1983. On the demise of Jack's, this one passed to Nationwide of Lanark for further service. Many of the other members of the fleet passed to Rennie's in the capacity of dealers.

Festival Travel were based at Kirkliston before relocating to Inverkeithing. School contracts have been built up in recent years. This view shows three ex-Lothian Dennis Tridents, and Bova Futura FHD12-340 VIL 8219. This was originally new to Jay Coaches of Greengairs as B1AFC, and is now a seventy-seater. It came from Travelstar European, where it was registered YS52 TSE and liveried for National Express, but it has also carried the registration SV04 GRF.

WCY 701 was a Neoplan N722/3/Plaxton Paramount 4000 CH53/18Ct, new as South Wales Transport number 153 in June 1986. On disposal, it became C357 KEP before joining Partridge of Hadleigh and then Heddingham and District (L228). It passed to Rennie's as PIJ 601, then on disposal became C137 BMS.

J2DTS was a Neoplan Skyliner N122/3 CH77Ct, purchased new by Durham Travel Services in November 1991. It passed to Moffat & Williamson in 1998 and was re-registered to YBK 159. It was on a visit to Glasgow when captured at Ibrox Stadium. On disposal it joined Prentice Westwood as YRR 436 and later IUI 2129.

TPD 113X was a Leyland Olympian ONTL11/1R/Roe H43/29F, purchased new by London Country as their number LR13 in May 1982. It passed to the Oxford Bus Co., then Beeston's of Hadleigh, before purchase by Rennie's in 2002, and was snapped on a football hire to Glasgow.

GSU 853T was a Leyland Leopard PSU3C/3R/Alexander T Type C49F, new as Central Scottish T371 in April 1979. It became Kelvin Central 2513 in 1989 before passing to Spencer's of Leven. It was caught resting between bingo contracts, with the North Sea in the background.

LCK 740 was a Leyland Titan PD3/4/Burlingham FH72F, purchased new by Ribble as their fleetnumber 1577 in August 1958. On disposal it passed to Shennan of Drongan, before joining Rennie's in December 1973. It later passed to Paul Sykes (dealer) in October 1974, and was then resold to Harkin's of Glasgow for further service.

GMS 277S was a Leyland Leopard PSU3E/4R/Alexander Y Type B53F new as Alexander (Midland) MPE 277 in January 1978. It passed to Kelvin Scottish as their number 1011 in June 1985. It was sold off prematurely as part of a cost-cutting exercise and was snapped up by Stagecoach for their Hampshire Bus subsidiary. It returned to Scotland to work for Moffat & Williamson in 1988, and was on a Glenrothes local route.

EWY 75Y was a Leyland Olympian ONLXB/1R/Roe H47/29F, new as West Yorkshire PTE 5075 in March 1983. It passed to A1 Service of Ardossan, and later to Stagecoach with the business. Allison's of Dunfermline purchased three Olympians (EWY74–76Y) from Stagecoach Western. This was the only one to be repainted, and it later went on to have a second life as a non-PSV with Fife Constabulary.

J28 UNY was a Leyland Tiger TRCL10/3RZ/Plaxton 321 C53F, purchased new by Bebb's of Llantwit Fardre in January 1992. It passed to Moffat & Williamson in 1994 and was visiting Edinburgh on a hire, carrying the registration number 121 ASV. Plaxton bought the rights for Duple bodywork for £4 million, and the Duple 320 was re-worked; twenty-five were built at Scarborough in 1989. The 321 was around £6,000 cheaper than the Paramount and was only available from the Kirkby dealership.

329 YFM was a Guy Arab IV 6LW/Massey H41/32F, purchased new by Chester Corporation as their number 29 in June 1962. It is seen with Rennie's at Cairneyhill depot, still in its original livery, but would receive a repaint in due course. On disposal it would see further service with Grayline of Clackmannan.

YJ54 BUP was an Optare Solo M880 B25F, delivered new to Rossendale Transport as their number 46 in September 2004. On disposal, it became Tate's Travel of Dewsbury number 1542. It is now with Bay Travel of Cowdenbeath, and looks extremely smart since a blue skirt has been added to the livery.

PBN 656 was a Leyland Titan PD2/37/MCW Orion FH35/27F, purchased new by Bolton Corporation as their number 138 in 1961. It passed to SELNEC PTE with the Bolton undertaking, but was never repainted. On disposal it passed to Morris Bros of Swansea before reaching Rennie's of Dunfermline.

TPJ 67S was Bristol LHS6L/ECW B35F, new as London Country BN67 in November 1977. On disposal it passed to Eastbourne Buses as their number 13, before purchase by Moffat & Williamson in 1991. It is shown passing through Dundee on the service to Cupar, but had yet to receive fleetnames. It would pass to MacEwan's of Dumfries in 1994 for further service.

R79 KSX was a Dennis Javelin/Berkhof Radial C53F, new to Lothian in May 1998. It was among the last coaches to be purchased as that side of the business was wound down. It passed to Rennie's of Dunfermline in January 2003 and was re-registered to A15 RNY. At the end of the year it returned to its original registration number. In June 2004, after barely eighteen months in the Rennie's fleet, it passed to Clarkson of Barrow and was re-registered UCE 836.

B509 UNB was a Leyland Tiger TRCTL11/3RZ/Plaxton Paramount 3500 C57F, new as Shearings of Altrincham number 509 in April 1985. It was purchased by Moffat & Williamson in 1989, and re-registered to BSK 790 in July 1991. It was climbing through Glencoe on a dismal day while working a Highland tour for David Urquhart.

JFG 358N was a Leyland Atlantean AN68/1R/East Lancs H45/28D, purchased new by Brighton Corporation as their number 58 in July 1975. It passed to Rennie's in 1987 and was working a local service in Dunfermline. The bus didn't keep this livery too long, as it was soon repainted into the mainly cream livery with red bands.

C771 OCN was an MCW Metrobus DR102/55 H77F, purchased new by Northern General as their 3771 in June 1986. On disposal in 2002 it passed to M & W and is seen in Glenrothes. Council policy regarding school buses in the area has dictated a single-deck fleet being used nowadays.

P778 BJF was a Volvo B10M-62/Caetano Algarve C49Ft, purchased new by McLean of Witney in January 1997. It joined Toolan's of Kinglassie in 2003, and was re-registered as TCZ 6277 in January 2004. The Algarve was the UK version of the Delta II body sold throughout Europe.

KYV 756X was an MCW Metrobus DR101/14 H43/28D, delivered new to London Transport as their M756 in February 1982, passing to the privatised Leaside Buses in September 1994. It became part of Arriva, seeing service in London, Herts & Essex, and Scotland West. It was loaned to McGill's of Greenock before purchase by Rennie's of Dunfermline in August 2002. It passed to Stagecoach Fife with Rennie's business in March 2008 and was allocated fleetnumber 15927, but went to Wigley (Carlton) for scrap in July 2008.

YBW 606R was a Bristol VRT/SL3/6LXB/ECW H43/31F, purchased new by City of Oxford as their number 459 in November 1976. It passed to South Midland, which later became part of Thames Transit, and is seen after sale to Moffat & Williamson in 1989 while still in Orbiter livery as it worked a local service in Glenrothes.

MX05 AHL was a Volvo B12M/Jonckheere C42Ft, purchased new by Shearings Holidays as their number 718 in March 2005. It passed to Hunter's of Sauchie, before sale to Merlin Travel of Dunfermline. It carried the registration number M70 RLN for a spell before reverting to its original plate. It is now part of the Bay Travel fleet.

FJ04 ESU was a Volvo B12M / Sunsundeguidi C49Ft, purchased new by Rennie's of Dunfermline in May 2004, and caught in Castle Esplanade in Edinburgh. It passed with the business to Stagecoach and was re-registered as HKZ 726 and allocated fleetnumber 53008.

UFX 523L was a Bedford YRT/Plaxton Elite C53F, purchased new by Rendell of Parkstone in July 1973. It later passed to Jack's of Cowdenbeath and was seen on a visit to Glasgow. It would pass to Rennie's and receive the black-and-yellow livery introduced in 1986.

N702 FLN was a MAN 11.190/Optare Vecta B42F, new as R&I Tours of Park Royal number 252 in September 1995. R&I were taken over by MTL London in June 1996 and later by Metroline, with this bus becoming number MV252. It passed to Moffat & Williamson in 2001 and was working in Glenrothes.

TMS 51P was a Leyland Leopard PSU5A/4R/Plaxton Supreme C55F, purchased new in September 1976, and seen working on the Dunfermline–Plymouth Express Service. It was later fitted with an updated Plaxton Supreme front panel and re-registered as YCR 874. Wilson's of Carnwath purchased it in 1985.

X2 JPT was a Volvo B7TL/ East Lancs Vyking H47/29F, purchased new by Walsh of Middleton, trading as JP Travel, in November 2000. It was acquired by Moffat & Williamson in 2004 for use on Glenrothes town service 4 to Collydean. It later passed to Rossendale Transport as their number 100 in 2007.

This was Rennie's Wellwood yard in September 2003, showing a nice selection of mainly ex-London buses, all painted in the all-over red livery of the day. Over the years the colour scheme has changed quite a few times, with maroon and cream, yellow and cream, red and cream, yellow and black, and blue and white all being chosen at some time or other.

HSF 307N was a Ford R1114/Plaxton Elite C53F, purchased new by Kingdom Coaches of Methil in January 1975, and is seen on a football hire to Glasgow. Plaxton launched the Panorama Elite at the 1968 Commercial Motor Show in London. This essentially set the basic design of British coaches for the next fourteen years. The Elite was updated and a mark II and III version appeared – all were available with bus-grant-specification front doors and interiors. To complement this, destination blinds were also available in both the front grille and on the roof or front dome for front radiator chassis grille.

NKU 152X was a Dennis Dominator DDA133/Alexander RH Type H46/32F, delivered new as South Yorkshire Transport number 2152 in January 1982. It was sold to Allison's of Dunfermline and passed, via Fife Scottish and a company near Doncaster, to Pilkingtons of Accrington. It was later re-registered as PIB 8076.

A158 XFS was a Volvo B10M-61/Van Hool CH48/10Dt, delivered new to Rennie's in May 1984 for use on their Anglo-Scottish service linking Scotland to the South West of England. This coach would later serve with Summerbee of Southampton, Darley Ford Coaches and Collin's of Northfleet. It has had various registration numbers, including FXU 355, A632 RTT, 282 GOT and A26 4TP.

SN53 AVT was a Transbus Dart SLF B42F, new as Lothian Buses number 100 in October 2003. It passed to Bay Travel in 2015 for use on their tendered services and was working on service 89 in Dunfermline bus station. The bus had a new Hanover LED destination display fitted, and was bound for Crossford.

A471/3HNC were a pair of Dennis Falcon/Northern Counties H47/37F, new as Greater Manchester PTE numbers 1471/3 in April 1984. The 10.5-metre-long Falcon V featured a compact Mercedes-Benz OM421 V6 engine, which was rated at 188 bhp and mounted at the rear of the air-suspended chassis, driving straight to the GKN rear axle via a Voith D851 automatic gearbox with integral retarder. Only six Falcon Vs were built – three for Manchester, two for Nottingham and one demonstrator, which was converted into a playbus.

PWB 658X was a Leyland Leopard PSU5C/4R/Duple Dominant IV C53F, delivered new to Rennie's of Dunfermline in April 1982. It was later re-registered as YFG 333, and then to MFS 390X, and was captured on a visit to Glasgow. Duple Bodies & Motors was formed in 1919 by Herbert White in Hornsey, London, and continued until July 1989, when the decision was made to close down the Duple operations.

SF07 ODH was a Volvo B12B/Van Hool T9 C49Ft, purchased new by MacPhail's of Salsburgh in May 2007. It is now a member of the smart Cowdenbeath-based Bay Travel fleet. The new T9 series was launched in 1995 and was a completely new body design. The new livery is based on the same pattern as that used by Bayliss of Deal.

LFR 131T was a Dennis Dominator DD110A/East Lancs H45/31F, new as Blackburn Transport number 131 in June 1979. It passed to Rennie's in 1986, and featured a Maxwell gearbox, which was unreliable to say the least. It was later loaned by a dealer to Western National during a bus strike in Plymouth, and was later used by Kelvin Central Buses as a source of spares.

SP59 BSX is an Optare Versa V1110 B38F, purchased new by Moffat & Williamson in September 2009, seen in Glenrothes. The Versa is manufactured by Optare at its Sherburn-in-Elmet factory. As of March 2016, over 750 had been produced.

Rennie's launched a network of local services in Fife against Fife Scottish, using quite a varied fleet of buses outshopped in a red-and-cream livery, not unlike that of Fife Scottish. Three vehicles are seen resting between duties in Dunfermline bus station.

SFS 159V was a Leyland Atlantean PDR2 / Alexander H47/32D built for Leyland Motors in 1972 as an experimental development vehicle. It was sold to Rennie's in January 1980, but not registered until April. It had been built alongside a batch of buses for Liverpool Corporation, and would later work for Truronian in Cornwall.

217 AJF was an AEC Bridgemaster/Park Royal H72R, new in September 1961 to Leicester City Transport as their 217. On disposal it passed to Foster of Dinnington before reaching Rennie's in March 1974. It later became a berry bus, which fortunately bought it enough time to be purchased for preservation. It once again sports Leicester livery.

YD02 PXN was a Volvo B12M/Van Hool T9 C49Ft, purchased new by Reay of Wigton in June 2002. It later worked for Simmonds of Botesdale and MacPhail's of Salsburgh. It is now P555 BAY and was captured in Edinburgh.

YJ61 MMX is an Optare Solo M950 B32F, purchased new in February 2012 and caught while working on the St Andrews town service. M&W was founded in August 1978, when the fleets of Williamson's of Gauldry merged with Moffat's of Cardenden.

WCO 733V was a Volvo B58-61/Caetano C53F, purchased new by Trathen's of Yelverton in March 1980. On disposal it passed to Whyte's of Newmacher and was painted in Stagecoach livery while on long-term hire. It later passed to Weir's of Clydebank and MacIntosh of Dalmellington, but it is seen much later in its life as SIL 6823 with St Andrews Coaches, while passing Glasgow Cathedral.

JCK 532 was a Leyland Titan PD2/12/Burlingham H33/28RD, purchased new by Ribble as their fleetnumber 1457 in July 1956, shown operating for Rennie's. H. V. Burlingham was a British coachbuilding business based in Blackpool from 1928 until 1960, when they were taken over by London-based rivals Duple Motor Bodies Limited. Duple initially renamed Burlingham as Duple (Northern) but, in 1969, they closed their Hendon factory and concentrated production in Blackpool. Duple coach bodies were built in the former Burlingham premises until Duple itself was liquidated in 1989.

MAX 335X was a Leyland Tiger TRCTL11/2R/Plaxton Supreme VI C53F, purchased new by Thomas of Clydach Vale in March 1982. It passed to Whyte's of Newmacher, then Bruce of Airdrie before joining Moffat & Williamson.

JGE 520T was a Ford R1114/Plaxton Supreme C53F, new to Gorman's of Dunoon in June 1979. It passed to Jack's of Cowdenbeath and was working on hire to the Scottish Bus Group during the Glasgow holidays. It worked for Rootham of Newcastle, before joining McKendry of Loanhead in 1993.

B187 CGA was a Volvo B10M-61/Berkhof Emperor CH48/12Ft, purchased new by Western Scottish as their KV187 in February 1985. It was re-registered as 13CLT for a spell, before becoming B550 EGG prior to disposal to Marbill of Beith. It passed to Irvine's of Law in 1992 and became 790CVD. It is shown with Rennie's as GDZ 3363 in the white-and-blue livery employed at that time.

GOG 548N was a Daimler CRL6/Park Royal H43/33F, delivered new to West Midlands PTE as their number 4548 in March 1975. It worked on loan to Eastern Scottish at Livingston for a few weeks, before passing to Moffat & Williamson, and is seen at Glenrothes. It would pass to Watermill of Fraserburgh for further service.

GTN 172N was a Bedford YRT/Plaxton Elite C53F, delivered new to Moordale of Newcastle in December 1974. It passed to Letham of Comrie and was on a football hire to Hampden Park in Glasgow. It passed to Rennie's of Dunfermline in 1987, and then to Fisher's of Dundee.

B121 WUV was a Leyland TNLXB2RR H44/26D, new as London Regional Transport number T1121 in November 1994. It soon passed to privatised Stagecoach Selkent, and was converted to single door in 1998. It was transferred to East Kent as their number 1181 in December 1997. It passed to Rennie's in December 2002 and then to Stagecoach with the business in 2008.

FJ59 APZ is a Scania K340EB4/Caetano Levante C49FLt, delivered new to Premier of Nottingham in October 2009. It is seen with Festival Travel passing through Cowdenbeath. It came from Simpson of Rosehearty, but has also worked for Lewis Coaches of Coventry and Coachmaster of Leicester.

NNA 134W was a Volvo Ailsa B55-10/Northern Counties H44/35F, purchased new by Greater Manchester PTE as their fleetnumber 1446 in August 1980. On disposal it joined City of Lancaster Transport and became number 446. It passed to Hall's of Kennoway and was on a hire to Glasgow. It would pass to M-Line of Alloa in 1993.

JSF 774T was a Bedford YMT/Plaxton Supreme C46F, new to Silver Fox Coaches of Edinburgh in December 1978. It passed to Anstruther Coaches and was used on a summer service that connected Glasgow to Anstruther Caravan Park on Saturdays. On disposal it passed to Moffat & Williamson, and later Irvine's of Law for further service.

L520 EHD was a DAF SB3000/Van Hool Alizee C51Ft, delivered new to Coupland & Cronin, trading as C & H of Fleetwood, in March 1994. It passed to Taphaul Coaches, owned by Thomas Malcolm, and was seen in Edinburgh. The coach and haulage company went bust in February 2000. This coach later passed to Andrew's of Tideswell, and then Fraser Eagle as 7529UK.

C305 ASP was a DAF MB200/Duple Caribbean 2, new to Bruce of Pitscottie in October 1985, and is seen on a visit to Aberdeen. In June 1983 Duple was sold to the Hestair Group, which had already acquired the long-established business of Dennis Brothers of Guildford. Duple was renamed Hestair Duple, and the Laser and Caribbean were given a facelift to try to improve their popularity.

PWB 659X was a Leyland Leopard PSU5C/4R/Duple Dominant IV, new to C53F Rennie's of Dunfermline in April 1982, and seen after collection from the coachbuilders at Blackpool Promenade. It would later become MSP 333, and then MFS 579X, and would see further service with Collins Coaches, Cambridge, before passing to Williams & Robinson, Scunthorpe.

MW15 LUX is a Volvo B11R/Plaxton Panther C46Ft, purchased new by Moffat & Williamson of Gauldry in May 2015. It was caught leaving Glasgow on a Glenton Holidays Select Tour. The Generation 2 Panther was launched at Euro Bus Expo at Birmingham in November 2010, and features the use of a stainless steel structure to resist corrosion and prolong vehicle life expectancy.

C449 CWR was a Volvo B10M-61/Plaxton Paramount 3500 C48Ft, purchased new by National Travel (East) as their number 449 in February 1986, passing to NTE Coaches Ltd in January 1987. On disposal, it joined Clyde Coast of Ardrossan, and was re-registered as 4505 RU in September 1988. It was changed to C372 MGB in 1989 and passed to Smart & Howieson, trading as Abbey Garage of Newburgh, in April 1990. This was changed to OCO 251 the following year, and again to C840 SSB before sale to Bure Valley Coaches in March 1993.

K806 NTJ was an Optare MetroRider B17F, purchased new by Merseyside (7806) in July 1993. It was photographed in Glenrothes on a local bingo contract service operated by Spencer of Leven. The Optare MetroRider was built by Optare between 1989 and 2000. They based the original design on the MCW MetroRider after Optare bought the rights following a decision by MCW to end bus production.

HSX 150X was a Bedford YNT/Plaxton Supreme C53F, delivered new to JK Moffat of Leven in October 1981. Most Bedford coaches were supplied in Scotland by SMT Sales & Service, based at Finnieston in Glasgow. The company was part of the SMT Group, which owned most buses in Scotland, but remained in private hands after the buses were nationalised in 1948.

JWL 993N was a Bristol VRT/ECW H43/34F, purchased new by City of Oxford as their fleetnumber 440 in April 1975. It became Devon General 950, before reaching Moffat & Williamson in 1987. It would later join Johnson's of Hodthorpe for further service.

This is a Leyland Leopard PSU5A/4RT/Plaxton Elite C55F, seen on a football hire at Parkhead, the home of Celtic FC in Glasgow. It was new to Rennie's in May 1975, and on disposal saw further service with William O'Neill of Greenock. It would return to Rennie's for a second time in June 1986.

OES 72R was a Ford R1114/Plaxton Supreme C53F, purchased new by Bruce of Pitscottie in February 1977. It is seen on a visit to Bellahouston Park in Glasgow. The Supreme was first built, on small chassis only, in 1974, replacing the Panorama. On full-sized chassis, it replaced the Panorama Elite in 1975, and was superseded by the Paramount in 1982/3. However, the Supreme continued to be built on the small Bedford VAS chassis until 1986.

329 YFM was an ex-Chester Corporation Guy Arab IV 6LW/Massey H41/32F, shown in full Rennie's livery. It would later pass to Grayline of Clackmannan. Despite the fact that their lorry division was performing well by 1960, Guy faced seemingly insurmountable financial problems. The failure of the Wulfrunian was a commercial disaster and the operation in South Africa was losing them £300,000 a year. By 1961, Guy had no choice but to enter receivership. Sir William Lyons, managing director of Jaguar, acquired the company for £800,000.

Hamish Gordon established his company in 1981 and continues to work from the original base in Leslie. 776 WME was a Leyland Royal Tiger B54-70/Roe Doyen C46Ft, purchased new by ABC Taxis of Guildford, trading as Blue Saloon, in August 1984. It passed to Hall's of Kennoway as B23 PGX and was later re-registered to YSU 572. It was bought by Gordon's in 1999, becoming B23 PGX again, and later joining Sim's of Burntisland.

SK52 USF was a Volvo B7TL/Alexander ALX400 H45/20D, new as London United VA307 in January 2003. It joined A1 of Methil in 2013, and was departing from Leven bus station on a school run. Fife Council usually have a clause in their school contracts specifying an age limit of fifteen years.

MUS 152P was a Leyland Leopard PSU3C/4R/Duple Dominant B53F, purchased new by Graham's of Paisley as their number S9 in January 1976. It passed to William's of Cross Keys in May 1990, Mott's of Aylesbury in May 1993, and Luton & District in July 1995. Spencer's of Leven then ran it between March and October 1996.

A335 YDT was a Volvo B10M-61/Jonckheere Jubilee C50F, purchased new by National Travel (East) in April 1994. It passed to West of Mitcham, becoming GSU387 on the way. Armstrong's of Inverkeithing acquired it in 1991 and re-registered it as HIL 5186; it was captured at Glasgow Green.

ATB 598A was a Leyland Atlantean PDR1/1/Weymann L39/34F, purchased new by Fishwick's of Leyland as their number 31 in November 1963. It passed to Rennie's in 1977 and was caught in Edinburgh. From 1964, a drop-centre rear axle was available as an option for the Atlantean and those with drop-centre rear axles became known as Atlantean PDR1/2s.

WUT 121X was a DAF MB200/Plaxton Viewmaster C53F, purchased new by Kirby Coaches of London SE5 in June 1982. It was purchased by Kingdom Coaches of Methil, marking a change in vehicle policy as it was a heavyweight chassis. The original livery was simply adapted and lettered up.

VYH 48G was a Leyland Atlantean PDR2/1/Roe H45/23F, new as Hall's of Hounslow number 69 in April 1969. On disposal it passed to Shennan of Drongan, Dougall's of Dundee, and Irvine's of Law, before reaching Moffat & Williamson in 1981 as an eighty-eight-seater.

AFC 498V was a Ford T152/Plaxton Supreme C35F, purchased new by Smith & Webb of Booker in October 1979. It passed to Williamson of Methil and is seen in the mustard livery adopted in the early 1970s.

H153 MOB was a Dennis Dart/Carlyle B28F, new as London Buses's DT153 in November 1990. It passed to London United in November 1994. Allison's of Dunfermline bought it in February 2000, and sold it with the business to Stagecoach Fife two months later. It was allocated the fleetnumber 691, and later 32343. In October 2003 it passed to Birmingham Motor Traction, who were in turn taken over by Flights Hallmark. In January 2007 it went to Trustline of Hunsdon, then Puma Coaches of Glasgow.

F95 CBD was a Volvo B10M-60/Jonckheere Deauville C50Ft, purchased new by Middleton of Rugeley in July 1989. It later served with Classic Coaches of Annfield Plain and Prentice Westwood. Over the years it carried many registration numbers, including YSV607, PR1767, and MBZ1758. On joining Hamish Gordon, it became B10 MHG. On disposal it passed to PJ Travel of Dalmuir.

GWV 930V was a Leyland Leopard PSU3E/4RT/Plaxton Supreme C48F, new as Southdown number 1330 in July 1980. It was one of thirty-six taken by Rennie's from Southdown, and was branded for the R22 service introduced in July 1989, linking Glasgow and Kirkcaldy. It was later sold to Suirway of Passage East in Eire and became 80-WD-225.

OSP 594J was a Bedford VAS5/Plaxton C29F, purchased new by Whitelaw's of Methilhill in October 1971, and was snapped on a hire to Glasgow. The Bedford VAS chassis made its debut at the 1960 British Commercial Motor Show, and was available with a 214 cubic inch petrol (VAS2) engine, a 300 cubic inch petrol engine (VAS3) or a 330 cubic inch diesel engine (VAS5). All engines were six cylinder.

GAX 569L was a Leyland Leopard PSU3B/2R/Willowbrook B53F, delivered new to West Monmouthshire as their number 18 in 1972. It later became Islwyn Transport number 18 and was sold to Rennie's in May 1987. This view shows it prepared for service at Cairneyhill depot.

A654 EMY was a Leyland Royal Tiger B54-62/Roe Doyen C47Ft, purchased new by National Travel (London) in May 1984. It passed to London Country (South West) as their DTL654 for use on Green Line services. On disposal it passed to Alpine of Llandudno, before joining Hall's of Kennoway.

R554 JDF was a Volvo B10M-62/Plaxton Premier 350 C49Ft, new as Cheltenham District number 554 in September 1997. It was transferred to Stagecoach North West and caught up in the Carlisle floods of January 2005. It passed to Davies of Plean, and then Taphaul Coaches of Cowdenbeath as CNZ2978. On disposal it joined Bennetts of Warrington, before purchase by Redline of Preston. It was re-registered as PJZ6442 and re-seated to C70F.

VMJ 959S was a Leyland Leopard PSU3E/4R/Plaxton Supreme C53F, purchased new by Plaskow & Margo of London, in September 1977. It passed to Moffat & Williamson, and was working for the Scottish Bus Group as a duplicate on their Glasgow–Blackpool service during the Scottish holiday season.

E748 HJF was a Dennis Javelin 12SDA/Plaxton Paramount C53Ft, built as a demonstrator for Dennis Specialist Vehicles, Guildford, in January 1988. It was purchased by Bruce of Pitscottie and was working on hire to Wallace Arnold on a feeder journey, taking passengers from Scotland to join their tours at Leeds.

Y188 CFS was a Dennis Dart SLF/Plaxton Pointer B42F, new as Lothian Buses number 188 in August 2001, but was renumbered as 53 when a 2013 Volvo B7RLE took on that number. It passed to Bay Travel and is seen in full livery, complete with blue skirt.

GMS 301S was a Leyland Leopard PSU3E/4R/Alexander Y Type B53F, new as Alexander (Midland) number MPE301 in April 1978. It was one of six acquired by Moffat & Williamson, but was involved in an accident in January 1992 and lay in storage for eighteen months. It is shown parked up at St Fort, awaiting a decision as to its future.

It was decided to rebuild GMS 301S and, at the same time, to update the styling to include a PS Type front end, and a squarer roof profile. The work was done by John McHardy Coachworks, who were based in Gauldry. The finished result is seen here before it re-entered service, but surprisingly the decision was taken not to re-register it.

LJS 841S was a Ford R1114/Plaxton Supreme C53F, purchased new by Newton's of Dingwall in August 1977. Anstruther Coaches were using it on their summer service from Glasgow to Anstruther Holiday Village. The location was Park's Independent Coach Terminal in Glasgow.

SN51 AXH was a Dennis Trident/Plaxton President H45/26F, purchased new by Lothian Buses as their fleetnumber 603 in November 2001. On disposal it joined Festival Travel of Inverkeithing for use on school contracts, and retains the harlequin livery applied by Edinburgh.

SN66 WHK is an ADL Enviro E20D MMC B30F, delivered new to Moffat &
Williamson in September 2016. It was captured in St Andrews working on the
92B service, bound for Tayport. The Enviro200 was originally designed to be
the replacement for the Dennis Dart SLF chassis and Alexander ALX200 and Plaxton
Pointer 2 bodies. In 2014, a third-generation version of the Enviro200 was launched,
known as the Enviro200 MMC, replacing the original design.

FJ57 KJO was a Scania K340EB4/Caetano Levante C49FLt, purchased new by
National Express as their fleetnumber SC41 in November 2007. It passed to Bay
Travel of Cowdenbeath, and is seen freshly repainted and lettered up.

PJH 456H was an AEC Reliance 6U3ZR/Plaxton Elite C53F, delivered new to Rowson of South Harrow in June 1970. It passed to Hall's of Kennoway and is seen in Glasgow while working the summer Saturday-only service to Anstruther Holiday Village.

NLS 250P was a Bedford SB5/Duple Dominant C41F, purchased new by Rennie's of Dunfermline in November 1975. The Bedford SB was launched at the 1950 Commercial Motor Show as the replacement for the Bedford OB. It was built for the UK market and export, and production spanned thirty-seven years, longer than any other Bedford bus chassis, until the sale of Bedford Vehicles in 1987.

MX06 ADO is an Optare Solo M880 B25F, delivered new to Moffat & Williamson in March 2006. It is seen working a local service in Glenrothes. It is believed that a clause in the take-over of James Moffat's business stipulated that his brown livery had to remain on some vehicles at least. Eventually the merged fleet settled on a brown-based livery as standard.

PO16 HSX is a MAN 19.290/MOBI People Explorer, new to Festival Travel of Kirkliston in March 2016. It is primarily used on Fife schools routes and is a seventy-seater; it is seen here in Inverkeithing. BASE Coach Sales, part of the Holmeswood Group based near Ormskirk in Lancashire, is the UK importer for the bus and coach products of MOBI. Based in Coimbra, Portugal, Mobi People is headed by Antonio Catarino, who previously held a senior position with Marcopolo, and even most of the workforce previously worked at the Marcopolo plant.

FSL 615W was a Bedford YLQ/Plaxton Supreme IV C45F, new to Henderson of Markinch, trading as Scotia Travel, in July 1980. It passed to West Coast Motors in 1985 and has survived into preservation. Bedford was a brand of vehicle produced by Vauxhall Motors, which was ultimately owned by General Motors.

XSA5Y was a Volvo B57-60/Alexander Y Type B51F, purchased new by Northern Scottish as their NA1 in March 1983. On disposal it passed to Rennie's and was captured in Dunfermline on a school contract. It later passed to D. P. Owens of Rhiwlas, and then WJC Coaches, but is sadly just rotting away at present.

RTF 561L was a Leyland Leopard PSU5/4R/Alexander M Type C46Ft, purchased new by Ribble as their 701 in December 1972; it was the only non-Scottish customer M Type built. It later passed to North Western and National Travel before sale to Black & White of Scunthorpe. It then worked for Whiteheads Coaches/Sports Tours of Rochdale before being taken by Rennie's as a trade-in. Here it was resting at Cairneyhill depot.

G887 VNA was a Scania K113CRB/Plaxton Paramount 3500 C53F, new as Shearings Holidays number 887 in April 1990. It passed to Reliable Vehicles (dealer) and went on hire to Dodd's of Troon in March 1995 for seven months, and then later to Silver Choice of East Kilbride. It joined the fleet of JM, AF, and DP Philp, trading as Allison's of Dunfermline in May 1996.

E997 NMK was a Leyland Tiger TRCTL11/3ARZ/Plaxton Paramount 3200 C55F, purchased new by Armchair of Brentford in April 1988. It was acquired by Moffat & Williamson in March 1993, and re-registered to FSU 374 a year later. Cowdenbeath provides the backdrop to this shot.

EWS 845D was a Leyland Titan PD3A/2/Alexander H41/29F, new as Edinburgh Corporation number 845 in July 1966. It passed to Williamson's of Gauldry and was initially used in its Edinburgh colours. It is shown in Cupar after a full repaint into the blue-and-cream livery used by Williamson's, and would last until 1983.

G844 GNV was a Volvo B10M-60/Jonckheere Deauville C51Ft, delivered new to Warner's of Tewkesbury in September 1989. It passed to Konect Bus and was re-registered as MIB 3378 in May 2001. Robinson's of Burbage purchased it before it reached MacMillan of Charlestown, trading as Living High Travel, in March 2005.

UWJ 888L was a Leyland Leopard PSU3B/4R/Duple Viceroy C53F, purchased new by Robert Hague of Sheffield in March 1973. It passed to Jack's of Cowdenbeath, and was snapped in Glasgow during the miners' strike of 1984. It would pass to Rennie's for further service in 1985.

KSA 179P was a Leyland Atlantean AN68A/1R/Alexander AL Type H45/29D, purchased new by Grampian as their number 179 in January 1976. Rennie's acquired it in 1987; at the time it was rumoured to be the precursor of a batch of ten. In the event it remained unique. Here it was working a local service in Dunfermline in Cowdenbeath.

VTX 428 was an AEC Regent V LD3RA/Weymann H37/33F, new as Rhondda number 428 in 1958. It passed to Williamson's of Gauldry in 1972 and ran until it lost its upper deck after an argument with Buffies Brae railway bridge in Dunfermline on 27 of October 1974, and had to be scrapped afterwards.

SN53 AVR was a Transbus Dart SLF B42F, purchased by Lothian Buses as their fleetnumber 99 in October 2003. On disposal it passed to Bay Travel, but has now moved on to Merlin Travel. Both operators work together and even share the same depot.

BHB 340C was a Leyland Titan PD3/4/East Lancs H41/32F, new as Merthyr Tydfil number 140 in June 1965, alongside ex-Fishwick Leyland Atlantean ATB598A at Cairneyhill depot. Opinion was divided in the early 1960s between the reliability given by front-engined chassis and, on the other hand, the seating capacity and suitability for driver-only operation afforded by rear-engine chassis.

B11 WGS was a Volvo B7R/Sunsundegui Sideral C40F, purchased new by Gordon's of Rotherham in March 2009. It passed to Moffat & Williamson and now carries the registration number 121 ASV. Sunsundegui was established in 1944 in Irún, Spain. Their main activity was the repair of wooden train wagons, primarily for RENFE (Spanish Railway Company). In 1987 the company got involved in the field of bus and coach bodywork building in Alsasua.

PHH 409R was a Bristol VRT/ECW H43/31F, purchased new by Cumberland as their number 409 in December 1976. It was transferred to Inverness Traction as their number 119 before purchase by Rennie's in November 1993. It was awaiting its next spell of duty at Wellwood depot.

MNU 193P was a Daimler Fleetline CRG6/Northern Counties H47/30D, new as City of Nottingham number 193 in March 1976. It was purchased by Moffat & Wiliamson in 1988, and was passing through Dundee while working on service X95 bound for St Andrews.

TRR 424X was a Volvo B10M-61/Plaxton Viewmaster C51F, purchased new by Neilson of Edwinstowe in May 1982. It was bought by Morley's Grey of West Row and, on their demise, passed to John Bruce of Airdrie. It was re-registered to 2190 RO in September 1986 and on disposal to Riddler's of Arbroath became HGD 829X. It passed to Irvine's of Law in 1993 and became TIB 2400. Surprisingly it returned to John Bruce in November 1993, and was then sold to Anderson of Lower Largo in March 1997.

BU04 UTF was a Mercedes Tourismo C49Ft built as a demonstrator for Evobus, Coventry, in June 2004. It is shown with Malcolm of Dysart, wearing the 'Premier Travel' brand. A loose alliance with Davies & Myles of Plean would see them also trade as Premier and help each other out with hires and vehicles. The Tourismo (also designated as the Mercedes-Benz O350) is an integral coach manufactured since 1994, and was initially manufactured in Hosdere, Turkey. In 2006 a revised version was launched and, by 2014, 21,000 had been sold.

SP54 FML is a Volvo B7R/Plaxton Profile C70F, purchased new by Moffat & Williamson in January 2005, and seen near St Andrews. The Plaxton Profile is built for the Volvo B7R and Dennis Javelin chassis. It is the smallest of Plaxton's full-sized coach range, and was the first Plaxton coach to meet DDA requirements by widening the entrance in order to fit a wheelchair lift.

MX53 ZWC was a Mercedes 0814D/Onyx C21F, new to Campbell's of Balloch, trading as Alexandria Coach Hire. It passed to McColl's Coaches before reaching A1 Coaches of Methil, and is seen outside the depot. As can be seen, the firm also supplies wedding cars.

LK03 NKD was a Transbus Trident H39/20D, new as Centrewest TN1278 in April 2003, but now with Bay Travel of Cowdenbeath. Ensign (dealer) up-seated it to H43/27F before it entered service. The livery on this vehicle has remained unique.

X705 UKS was a Dennis Dart SLF/Plaxton pointer B29F, purchased new by Stuart Shevill, trading as Stuart's of Carluke, in January 2001. It would later pass to Moffat & Williamson in November 2001 for further service, and was working on a Glenrothes local route.

M106 PRS was a DAF SB3000/Caetano C53F, purchased new by Whyte & Urquhart of Newmachar in September 1994. It passed to Toolan's of Kinglassie in 1999, and was working for Caledonian Travel when snapped in Falkirk.

TTB 974 was an all-Leyland Titan PD2/12, purchased new by Fishwick's of Leyland as their fleetnumber 14 in August 1954. It was sold in February 1973 and passed to Rennie's of Dunfermline. Fishwick's had many dealings with Rennie's over the years, as both were committed Leyland users.

NK51 ORL was a Scania K124/Van Hool C44Ft, new as Durham Travel Services of Hetton-le-Hole number 34 in October 2001. It passed to Highwayman of Errol, before joining Malcolm of Dysart. It would later pass to PMJ Travel, and Ogden's of St Helens as R60J DO. It was snapped on a hire to Glasgow with its Premier branding applied.

SSP 142K was a Leyland Leopard PSU3B/4R/Plaxton Elite C53F, purchased new by Rennie's of Dunfermline in January 1972. It later passed to William O'Neill of Greenock. The Leopard was Rennie's chosen vehicle at the time, as it was a very reliable chassis that had been in production for many years.

C356 FVU was a Leyland Tiger TRCTL11/3RZ/Caetano Algarve C51Ft, purchased new by Smith's of Wigan in May 1986 for use on National Express work. It passed to Moffat & Williamson of Gauldry for further service, becoming 121 ASV in the Fife-based fleet. Only seven of this combination were ever bodied and Smith's took three of them – subsequently all three passed to Moffat & Williamson.

VSC 337V was a Bedford VAS5/Duple Dominant C29F, purchased new by Jack's of Cowdenbeath in June 1980, and seen here scurrying through Dunfermline. It would later pass to Area Rural Transport in Leicestershire for further service.

X594 USC is a Dennis Trident/Plaxton President H47/24D, purchased new by Lothian Buses as their 594 in October 2000, although later converted to single door. It is now in the fleet of Bay Travel and is seen in Cowdenbeath, looking superb.